WILD FAMILIARS

New Women's Voices Series, No. 188

poems by

Linda Malm

Finishing Line Press
Georgetown, Kentucky

WILD FAMILIARS

ACKNOWLEDGMENTS

Taos Journal of Poetry ~ Kairos
Adobe Walls: An Anthology of New Mexico Poetry Volume 2 ~ "Corbie's";
    Volume 3 ~ "Autumn Pond"
Sugar Mule: Woman Writing Nature ~ "Loon" and "Losing"
Winded from the Chase ~ "A Thing with Feathers;" "As if I Would Forget;"
    "Crow Familiar"
Howl: University of New Mexico Anthology ~ "Child Song"
Waywords ~ Excerpted from "The Scale of Things"

Publisher: Leah Huete de Maines
Editor: Christen Kincaid
Cover Art: Charles Kohlhase
Author Photo: Donn Young
Cover Design: Elizabeth Maines McCleavy

Order online: www.finishinglinepress.com
    also available on amazon.com

Author inquiries and mail orders:
Finishing Line Press
PO Box 1626
Georgetown, Kentucky 40324
USA

Contents

For Donn Young

Kairos

What am I but autumn passing. I face late
sun, enjoy the warmth. Know my long shadow

drops behind. A troubadour twangs: Leaving you was easier—
I lower the volume. In the pond-side chair my posture shifts.

Few find passion in the crowded years of toiling.

Daylight slants and stars veer according to the season.
Old age comes with force

and fascination. It asks me to give
meaning to where I am. I hear parting wingbeats

across the pond. I see others join
                        above the river, woods, and fields.

If you ask me for the cost of life I've given to be
with this land

I'll tell you I lived long enough.
The price of stewardship was fair.

Autumn Pond

How does one act against the flame
flashed from a rufous hummingbird, or
iridescent dragonfly lighted on a lily pad?

The pond, a sunken socket. Blue eye
still out stares the drying sun.

Trout rise to glide like birds in skies
of limpid water. Reflections of the piney hills
wobble with each swallow swoop.

A Nighthawk pair screech and veer.
Chevroned wings slice dusk.

Loon

Hysterical black call—

        tremolo half-laugh carves into fog.

Solitary longing song—

        wail echo skims the miles of water.

Another deep dive search—

        a sudden silent lake.

Elusive and emerged again—

        Loon, I solo too.

Shadowing

I'm lost in watching every far-flung flake
wayward lilt and white melt into drizzle.
No imprint on the thawing pond.
Trout drift, gills fan the only current.
They've no more sense of Spring than troubled sky.

But pond, your moods can muddle day, distract
my melancholy. I see through your eye.
Ripples blur like tears. Trees diffuse.

When windless clouds glow plum
and umber, time seems languid. Days lengthen.
The South sends forth the glistening dragonfly.
Between greening willows mallards choose.
New pairs glide.
O
for such a shadowing.

Trilling

Opening the morning door
unmuffling a house wren
trilling for a mate.
Mouth an open vee.
Canted tail, a checkmark
above his offering stuffed
inside the birdhouse.
Twigs splayed like sketch marks
beckoning her come in.

I step outside to meet my wren.
He pauses, as if I were
his heart's desire
and in that moment—O
if I could be in harmony
poem to song
sharing expectation.

He spills with melody again.
I look into the landscape,
hoping she's out there
bright-eyed in a nearby tree
delayed by just competing
notes of wind or water.
On her way, but only
after preening, then dining
on a beetle and some seed.

Entrapment

A summer breeze slips up slope.
Shore birds slide the cliff face, rise
though one first flails, then falters,
wound with filament
caught while seizing fishing bait.
He made an easy catch, now
becomes one.

I clasp him in my arms.
Wild wings wrap my shoulders
more widely than expected.
Faint body heat through feathers.
Breast beats against breast.
His fearsome beak beside my neck
curious and gentle—

and I am lovely
Leda, languidly unwinding
enmeshed in softest white.

Release with great delight.

A Thing with Feathers
—Emily Dickinson

Captured, carried in a purse, sold for a twenty.
Cage set on a check out counter.
Labeled Amazon Double Yellow Head.
My breed smiles where our beak halves meet.
Our wide-eyed gaze fixes and beguiles.
The pet store owner proffers
Some say they live to be a hundred.

Two hundred dollars later I am
Miller, (named after Henry).

In time I molt my first wing feather,
crane my head down to retrieve it,
place it in her hand. Luminescent.
Her nail lightly taps my beak.
She has seen me tear quickly into things,
exert three hundred pounds of pressure.
Riding her shoulder, I lightly preen her ear.

I squawk if my cage is left in the kitchen
when company comes.

I'm a social bird. I join in. Embarrass her
by chuckling when I hear her manneristic laugh.
My first words were a honeyed, *Hello Miller*
heard every time she came home from work.
I softly repeat it when left alone looking
out the window. I add a robin's mating call.
Mimic the doorbell. I once cawed crow.

Sometimes I perch on her forefinger, thumb
clamped on my two front toes.
Her arm whirls to let me flap my wings.
She would never clip them. She likes to
press her ear against my chest to hear
the whirr of my two chambers.

She has two hearts.
Outside, I ride her wrist, rawhide
lace tied to my leg, one end to her finger.

And so, it was one jungle-humid day
the tall palm tree above us filled
with free parrots come to roost, a cacophony
of African and Amazon like me, some escaped
and some born free. Raucous squawks, song bird calls,
words like *hi honey, stop it—stop it,* a dog yip,
Japanese and Spanish—a clear coloratura.

She is amused, but I already feel among them.
I crane my neck, aim an upturned eye,
then look at her and she at me.
I shift my weight to one leg,
quickly beak the tie undone. I must have always
known how to do it. Rawhide dangles from her finger.
I crane my neck again. Look to the restless tree.

She strokes my soft breast feathers.

Raises her hand.

She whirls her arm without clamped thumb.

I lift.

We let go.

Your Voice on the Phone

A bird striking the window
Blue pansies flutter
from some sudden gust.

As If I Would Forget

A murder of crows assail the rare Buteo Regalis,
solitary hawk, but for this agitation.

She emits an unfamiliar melancholy whistle
veers and banks between hillside and sun.

Oscillating light pierces long slim wings.
Fra Angelico's pale ideal of angel.

       Suddenly

without wing beat, Regalis slices
through the cloudless sky until

       a dot.

That night a meteor at light-years end
cuts a burning arc into the hill.

Crow Familiar

Crow cacophony
black sky spirals
cause unknown

Our memorized landscape
I seek
What can be different?

Fresh kill?
Song dog? Hawk? Cat?
crow confusion

Then I too spy
the glint of gloss
in matt gold leaves

Once we watched each other.
this last fibrillation
leaves an empty chamber.

breath-less corridor
behind the beak
black frozen cry

Long clawed toes grip-less,
rumpled feathers
touched

there is no denying
my lost spirit-lifter
a hunger I can't feed.

furtively I take my crow
my wild familiar.
My honored feather cache.

Suddenly a silent sky
tail, head, wing shafts—
four-ray stars.

fold and fall
crows like cinders
catch in limbs.

When time in time
unwinds my crow
I'll make a flute

carve space holes,
blow breath
through a hollow wing bone.

play diminuendo with
whap/whap/woof of wingbeats
to shadows whirled on mine.

Levitation

The Cat Flattens
                    leaps

            snaps the hummingbird's feet
            dangling wires left for legs
            gorget flashing iridescent red
            diabolic sun play

The Cat Yowls

            wing blurs hover
                            humming Z's
            across my reddish shirt
                        won't
                            slow
                                won't
                                    leave
                                        my bosom
                                            won't end
the honeysuckle nectar-burn
                                frenetic buzzes
                                z
                        z
                z
pierce my heart.

                        Torpor come. Come.
                        I'll powder him with pollen dust,
                        wrap him in a petal shroud,
                        redolent scent.

The Cat Waits

Stop bird.

Stop.

Mercy.

Stop.

Let us be quieted.

Gone

Below a flowering branch
a hummingbird feeder glows.
Tail light in low sun.

Ropes and Spaces

I swing face down in the hammock.
A shaft of penstemon waves—red
Devil, back and forth behind the tree.
My rocking boat of rope and spaces
provides a snaky view of tickly grasses,
scratchy ground. Fierce fire ants
ignore my shadow scythe. Branch
patterns swathe across my back, sweeping
swift and steady as a hunting hawk.

…a way to go.

At a sharp turn on the trail
a long-wing swish across
the shoulder of the hill.

No shocked screech,
but a limp quail dropped,
still, but for a rapid flow
of glistening blood
from eight decisive
talon pierces.

I pass.

Pain-free prey
gripped and lifted.

Reclaimed sustenance.

Still Life

Caught in a lightening lunge for prey
a kestrel with a grosbeak in its grip
crashes my window.

He must have seen the holographic bird tape
but lunged too fast to lift.

I study hooked beak, drill-hole nostrils,
razor talons. The grossbeak's stocky beak
bleeds from a gash, toes clenched like fists.

Unnatural scrutiny.

Blue-gray sickle wings and chunky black and white ones
Russet back, cream speckled breast contrast with
black-white-orange harlequin effect.

Wild feathers are seduction.

I can't let these go. Place predator and prey together,
stone weight wing spreads. Seal the box,
not knowing mites eat both flesh and feathers.

Months pass before I peer inside again.

Alarmed at deeper seeing.

Fragile wings are ivory fans. Each skull—a fetish.

Canticle

Frail ghostly mobile
bird bones striking together
both tinkle and toll.

Beyond Books and Binoculars

Spring flight ecstasy! Self-made breeze and glide
until air turns glass.

A robin thuds to earth.

The angle of the glance, a breastbone strong from tireless
flight, perhaps protection. Light lift and fall of breath.

Askew. Up righted, reassembled, his head sags on my thumb.
Deep loss of time, abandoned instinct.

A hawk cries overhead.

Robin's tongue pulls in. Pinched beak.
Eye blinks. Increased warmth. His pulse or mine?

Tightened grip. Hot expulsion. All systems go.
A look left. A look right. None at looming me. A thrust.

I fly as he rises to a tree.

Not Yet Singing

Fledglings so full of heart
the nest fibrillates.

Down fluffed heads
dark beady eyes
beaks split with each
sharp arrival note
of a fleeting parent.
Another folded bug
caught mid-flight,
plunged down a
pink insistent throat.

Offspring and parent
fiercely single-minded.

Child Song

While her mother cleaned Xhemena
shyly crouched beneath the dining table,
thin-limbed grasshopper-folded child
fingering a stiff pink pocketbook,
sucking from a purple juice container.

In time she regularly retrieved
the downy chick and plushy rabbit
stowed in a closet
(sentiments from men who wished
more child in me than was remaining.)

Today Xhemena's fingers typed across
my cluttered desktop—scurrying brown sand crabs.
I snapped!—a hungry gull!
Giggles...... ...... then we fell still.
(Perhaps because we shared no common language.)

Then Xhemena pressed against me
and my arm
        dropped
                like an old hen's wing
                to make a downy heartbeat place.

Widow's Letter To Her Daughter

Today—the gift of a lifetime, a flicker and her
fledglings and then a towhee counting his feathers.
Cardinals were whistling from deep in the woods.

In time to come, earth may be bleaker
but for now, swamp maples have turned scarlet.

What a bludgeoning sight, and then you call to top it all
off like a big dollop of cream on a banana split sundae.

Love,
      the unalterable kind.

          Your Mum

Losing

A mumuration
of ominous starlings alights.

                      Black turns iridescent.

A gyring hawk
 drops a sharp wing feather.

                      Wind quiver.

You are in Nature's sight.

                      I am ready to be wounded.

Omen

Outside the empty
feeders taunt the winter birds.
Inside, someone's sick.

Abrupt Turn

I push a shopping cart down a wide aisle
while searchlights sweep over tall shelving
but there is nothing to buy or return.

A bird flies into my basket, skids to a landing,
cocks a foot back like a champion skater
almost finessing a too-abrupt turn.

I'm wheeled on a gurney, medivacked to the city.
I say that I'd rather be rushed to Hawaii.
I want to see inside mountains that burn.

A face above me says sorry, no time. I skid
to a landing, cock a foot back like a champion skater
almost finessing a too-abrupt turn.

My heart is a bag of rubbery pulses,
my lifeline reduced to a wavy green line.
The doctor declares no long-term concern.

A bird flies through tangles of tubing into my hand,
cocks a foot back like a champion skater
finesses an abrupt turn.

Behind the School Bus

Heads silhouetted, perched like crows
balanced on the seat back rows,
until the bus without concern
makes a haughty high rump turn,
lunch box cage rattling kids about.

Red flashing stop. They flutter out.

Crow Visitation

A crow, slicked and dressed in customary
black, perches close beside me
musing on my log this morning.

I listen to her cadence and off key pitch,
a rodent, bready, buggy conversation
with flock and nesting details.

So intimate, I forsake caution,
lean to touch the deep blue
sun glint on her back.

Rowing wing beats. Waiting wind.
Clouds hasten her disappearance.

Feather in my path.

Corbies

1

Swerve! Six flighty crows
flock to their nervous work—
road kill removal.

2

I heard two ancient Corbies' plight
Sall we dine? There lies slain knight
I'll pike his bonnie eens once bright.

3

I wonder if the blackbird singing
in the dead of night spoke
Olde English to his carrion delight.

4

Crow footprints
in the corners of my eyes.
Marking time.

5

No shooting limit.
Is that why a flock of crows
is called a murder?

6

Crows in my cornfield.
Black frocked inspectors swagger,
wings behind their backs.

7

I'm angry at their cawing.
They mock my scary straw man.
I'll bar their prying up my corn.

8

I vow they'll eat crow instead.
No more rowing wing-beats
as the crow flies.

9

Suddenly there comes a tapping.
A visitation. Bird of yore.
He speaks in cautious cadences
In caws that I deplore.
I couldn't know his message
but suspect what he implored:
don't ponder trapping plans.
(I've sensed this plea before.)
Then he leans much closer,

quoath quite clearly, *Never more.*

Span

Silhouetted cormorant
silent in a bare drowned tree
Dinosaur revealed.

The Scale of Things

I dream Saturn rolls toward me,
rock and ice rings wheeling like birds.

Nebula mesh like clouds of snow,
stars and space fold into each other.

We are stardust in motion.

Linda Malm has a BA in English and Art History from Tufts University, and an MFA in Television and Film and an EdD in Higher Education Administration from UCLA. She taught English at every grade in public schools under Title 9 anti-discrimination Federal grants, then was an assistant professor at Cal Poly Pomona, a California State University, and an Associate professor at the Claremont Colleges. She taught television and film production, film history and communication courses at the university level until she became the Dean of Arts at Pasadena City College.

After retirement she moved to Taos New Mexico where she renewed her childhood interest in writing poetry. She completed numerous university courses, workshops and several intensive mentorships. The goal was to more fully understand contemporary poetry.

Linda is a Master Gardener and served as president of the Taos chapter of the Native Plant Society. She still enjoys some gardening and does swim. Her gourmet cooking has simplified.

Linda now summers in Taos, adjacent to Carson National Forest and winters adjacent to the Chihuahuan Desert Peaks Organ Mountain wilderness in Las Cruces. She has an interest in architecture and designed both compounds. The influence of both these natural environments is evident in the imagery that predominates both her chapbooks.

Among her philanthropic interests is the Toivo Malm trail system, named for her father. It boarders the Rio Grande River, starting at a recreationally underserved area of Alamosa, Colorado and ending at the Alamosa National Wildlife Refuge. There is a pedestrian bridge honoring her sister and trails named for her first-grade friend, her mother and for her husband. She has also endowed a free Thursday program named for her mother at her home town art museum in Fitchburg Massachusetts.

In 2023 Linda married her longtime companion, Donn Young.